Scientific Notes
for Sight-Reading and Ear Training

**Mnemonics for Musicians
- and Music Theorists -
of All Levels**

Paul Masterdon

Copyright © 2025 Paul Masterdon
All rights reserved.

No part of this publication may be reproduced, stored in a retrieval system, stored in a database and / or published in any form or by any means, electronic, mechanical, photocopying, recording or otherwise, without the prior written permission of the publisher.

This system is copyright protected.

First published 2025 by Cosmic Jive Publishing

www.cosmicjivepublishing.com

info@cosmicjivepublishing.com

Print version
ISBN 978-1-918219-16-6

Treble Clef Notes for Sight-Reading
ISBN 978-1-918219-04-3

Bass Clef Notes for Sight-Reading
ISBN 978-1-918219-03-6

More instrument-specific guides coming soon

About the Author

The author is a UK-based music educator with a passion for making learning fun and accessible. With years of experience teaching students of all ages, they've discovered that the best way to master music is by engaging the imagination—because when learning feels like play, the notes just stick.

When not crafting quirky mnemonics or demystifying sheet music, they can usually be found tinkering with half a dozen instruments, drinking far too much tea, and insisting that yes, even you can sight-read.

This book is their way of sharing the shortcuts, tricks, and "aha!" moments that turn frustration into fluency—one silly mental image at a time.

Introduction

Tired of forgetting which C is which? Here's the fun and creative way to finally make sense of all those note names — and remember them for good.

This book uses simple, vivid mnemonics to help you instantly recognize notes by their scientific pitch names. Perfect for singers, players, producers, and anyone who wants to finally make sense of which A or C they're talking about. You'll learn faster, remember longer, and never mix up your octaves again.

(And yes — these same mnemonics can also help train your ear if you want to go further — but we'll focus on that in another book.)

🧠 The Imagination Machine

Most people think learning note names means endless drills or flashcards. But your brain doesn't love dry data — it loves stories. Give it "C4," and it shrugs. Give it an exploding crimson castle, and suddenly it lights up.

This book turns those abstract letters and numbers into pictures, characters, and tiny stories that make remembering scientific note names natural and fast.

🔓 Unlock the Map of Sound

This isn't about memorizing for the sake of theory. It's about giving you a clear, visual map of sound — so you always know where you are in the musical landscape.

"High C" or "low C" only gets you so far. When someone says, "Start on A," you shouldn't have to ask, "Which one?" With this book, you'll finally have that clarity. You'll be able to:

- Instantly tell which octave a note belongs to.
- Visualize your voice or instrument across the full range.

- Communicate clearly with others — and with your DAW, tuner, or notation software.
- Build a deep sense of how sound is structured — note by note, octave by octave.

Once you master these mnemonics, you won't just know *it's a C* — you'll know it's C4, the "middle" of your musical world. That's when pitch names start to make sense — every note becomes part of a beautifully organized picture.

🕹 Your Cheat Code for Note Clarity

Think of scientific pitch notation as your musical GPS. Each note name tells you where you are — not just what note it is. The mnemonics make learning feel more like playing than studying — because that's what makes memory stick.

🔬 Why Mnemonics Work

Your brain struggles with abstract symbols like ♩ or C5 — but it's brilliant at remembering the vivid, the funny, and the emotional. By pairing each note with:

- a name ("Elf" for E4),
- a colour (Emerald for E), and
- a story and image (an elf in a scientist's lab coat watching channel E4 on TV),

you give your brain multiple anchors to grab onto.

More mental hooks = faster recall.
More senses = stronger memory.

That's why these silly, colourful associations work — they connect visual, verbal, and emotional systems in your brain all at once.

(And if you do want to use them later for ear training, you'll already have a head start — your brain will know where each note "lives.")

🎵 Why B4 Isn't the Same as B5

There may only be seven letter names, but each octave has its own personality.

* B3 feels warm and grounded.
* B5 sparkles and soars.

Without context, "B5" doesn't mean much. But "The Bee Note," buzzing high through the air — that sticks. Give that bee a hive that rhymes with 5 and it doesn't take a lot of effort to remember where B5 is on the music map.

By giving every note its own colour, character, and mood, you make the abstract concrete. You're not adding complexity — you're creating clarity. Your mind begins to *feel* where each note sits, even before you play it. That's the real power of mnemonics: they turn music theory into a mental landscape you can actually explore and recall — on paper, in your head, and on your instrument.

🎼 Why Learn Scientific Note Names?

If you've ever looked up your vocal range or seen a piano roll labeled with notes like C4 or A5, you've already met scientific pitch notation (SPN). It may sound technical, but it's one of the simplest and most useful systems in all of music.

SPN gives every note a clear address — a letter name (A, B, C…) paired with a number that tells you which octave it belongs to. Think of it as a musical postcode system:

C3 - the C one octave below middle C
C4 - middle C — the center of a piano keyboard
C5 - the C one octave above middle C

Once you learn these names, the musical map stops feeling abstract. You'll see and feel where you are — whether you're singing, playing, producing, or composing.

🎯 The Focus of This Book

This book focuses specifically on mnemonics for the scientific note names — the letter–number combinations themselves. It's designed to make them easy to visualize, recall, and use across every musical context.

It fits into my wider complete *Music Mnemonics* System for musicians, which includes:

- **Sight-Reading Mnemonics** – to help you read and remember notes on the treble and bass clefs effortlessly.
- **Instrument Mnemonics** – to connect those same notes physically on your instrument through fingering hacks.
- **Ear Training Mnemonics** – to develop pitch awareness through story and imagery.

This book is the SPN layer of that system. It complements the others beautifully — but it also stands strong on its own. If all you want is to finally understand the "C4" world and never mix up your octaves again, this book gives you that power in a fun, memorable way.

🧩 How It All Connects

Each book in the series uses consistent colours and character names — so once you learn one layer, the others become easier to absorb. For example:

- The Castle note appears in your sight-reading book as the name for Middle C.
- Here, the scientific version, C4., becomes the "Scientific Castle," complete with its own image and story.
- The Castle note shows up in your instrument-specific book/s with hacks to remember fingering for C4.

Each layer speaks to a different part of your musical brain: visual (notation), spatial (instrument), and conceptual (SPN). Together, they build a complete mental map — a mnemonic universe for music.

💡 Why SPN Matters

Even though SPN often hides in the background, it solves real, everyday problems:

- Clarity – No more "Which C?" confusion. "C4" says it all.
- Communication – It's a universal reference used in DAWs, tuners, and sheet music apps.
- Range awareness – Knowing your range as *A3–E5* helps you choose keys intelligently.
- Instrument connection – You can instantly match written pitch to your instrument's layout.
- Collaboration – SPN bridges instruments, singers, and software — everyone speaks the same language.

And once these names become second nature, your sense of pitch turns spatial — you start to *feel* where notes sit, not just on the page, but in the air and under your hands.

🌈 A Quick Word About Ear Training

Although this book isn't primarily about ear training, these mnemonics naturally help your ear along the way. When your brain links a sound to a colour, story, or image, you start to "hear" with context.

If you want to go deeper into that skill, my dedicated Ear Training Mnemonics book (coming out late 2025) expands this visual–auditory approach in full. But here, our mission is clear: to make the scientific note names stick — vividly, playfully, and for life.

🚀 How to Use This Book: Your Fast Track to SPN Mastery

You're about to train your eyes, ears, hands, and imagination to speak the same musical language — the language of scientific note names.

Each page introduces you to a note with:

- a name (like the Castle note for middle C),
- a colour, **c**rimson for C
- a number (its octave, like C4), and
- a mini-story and image that helps your brain lock it in.

These aren't random associations. They connect directly with the mnemonics in my other books — so if you've already met these characters, you'll recognise them instantly. Here, they simply put on their lab coats and join the world of scientific pitch notation.

If this is your first of my books, don't worry — everything stands alone. You'll learn every note and number through vivid imagery that makes them impossible to forget.

Step 1: 🎨 See It — and Feel It

- Look closely at the note's illustration, then make it come alive in your mind as if it's a scene from a film. The more vivid, the better.
- Next, watch it come alive on the staff where it lives.
- Now imagine your fingers used to hit that note on your instrument, (or voice), glowing with the note's colour. Bring that vivid image and overlay it onto your instrument. Let only the keys used for the note be involved in the scene. Picture the number as part of the image — maybe written in the air, on a flag, or glowing on the character's costume.

You're wiring together sight, movement, and imagination — your brain's favourite memory trio. You no longer have to grind away burning the midnight oil to remember facts: the info goes in effortlessly through play.

Step 2: 📢 Say It Loud

Speak the note clearly and with character. For example: "E! ... E4! ... The Elf Note!" Add some flair — sing it, shout it, even whisper it dramatically. The sillier you are, the more your memory locks it in. By saying the name, number, and mnemonic together, you activate multiple memory systems at once: verbal, emotional, and physical.

💡 Tip: If you're using my other books, always say the *full phrase* that goes with each mnemonic to help the auditory part of your brain file it in the right place and reinforce the visuals. You want only to associate '4' with the SPN note - not the 4th line of the staff, or the 4th fret of a guitar, etc.

Don't worry — your brain won't get the Elves mixed up. As each version of the mnemonic has its own image and context, your mind files them in separate, albeit linked, mental folders. And likewise, the Elves helping you find those notes on your instrument are also distinct!

Instead of blending the "E4"s together, your mind makes:

- one memory for the Scientific Elf (wearing a lab coat)
- one for the Sight-Reading Elf running on the staff's 1st line.
- And another for an Instrument Elf zip-wiring along the 1st string of a standardly-tuned guitar.

They're connected (all Elves = all the same note), but they live in different neural networks. This avoids confusion and makes recall faster, because your brain can jump straight to the right image depending on context.

The awesome thing is that your brain also knows they're all Elves so 'secretly' hardwires connections to the others. Therefore, when you play with one Elf, you effortlessly revise all the Elf's siblings — ear training, finger placement, sight-reading Elves — making your learning stratospherically fast.

What normally takes years (and some musicians never master ear training) is reduced to weeks, making you a better musician: faster and with a better appreciation of music.

Step 3: 🎹 Play, Picture, Imagine

Now, play that note on your instrument (and when away from it, visualise playing it) thinking of the vivid image.

- See the Elf rise with the sound from your instrument.
- Feel the glow of its colour as you play or sing.
- Picture its science number as part of the scene

This playful step links theory, sight, and touch. You're not just memorising; you're *anchoring* the note in multiple ways your brain understands.

Step 4: 🔄 Mix and Reinforce

Once you've met a few notes, test yourself:

- Say a number (like "E3") and try to visualise its character and place on the staff and your instrument
- Shuffle through the notes out of order.
- Visualise notes that are not in your instrument's range on a piano - it's an easy way to 'see' where they live.

Step 5: 🌟 Connect It All

When you start combining these notes, you'll notice something cool — they begin to form a world. Each octave feels like a new layer of that world.

That's how pitch begins to make sense spatially, not just intellectually. You can stop here if your goal is to memorise SPN — or, if you want to take it further, you can link what you learn here to:

- Sight-reading mnemonics (for instant staff recognition)
- Instrument mnemonics (for fingering and sight-reading)
- Ear training mnemonics (for sound recognition)

Everything connects. Each book builds on the same cast of musical characters, colours, and visual stories. Together, they form a complete mnemonic universe — but each piece works perfectly on its own.

🎯 The Sharps and Flats

Once you've mastered the natural notes, it's time to meet their cousins — the sharps (♯) and flats (♭). It's tempting to think of them as "C plus a bit" or "E minus a touch," but that slows your brain down. Instead of *translating* from one note to another, train your mind to see every sharp and flat as its own distinct identity.

Each one deserves its own image and character twist. The more personality they have, the faster you'll recall them.

🏰 Sharps: Think Up, Think Edge

A sharp note sits just above its natural version — higher, brighter, a touch sharper in both sound and personality. To make sharps memorable, 'see' your mnemonic character gaining energy or an edge:

- Your Castle (C4) becomes the Sharp Castle (C♯4) — its turrets gleaming, flags pointed like arrows, maybe a lightning bolt striking the tower.

- The Elf (E4) becomes E♯4 — holding sharp scissors while assisting Santa wrapping sharp gifts.

Think "rightward" on a piano, "upward" in sound, "sharper" in vibe. Make them sparkle, glint, or bristle with that extra tone of intensity.

🍌 Flats: Think Down, Think Smooth

A flat note sits just below its natural version. Your mnemonic could look literally "flattened" in a cartoony way, could be depressed, or just see it mellowing out:

- The Castle (C4) becomes C♭4 — bulldozed flat.

- The Armadillo (A2) becomes A♭2 — roadkill in a Roadrunner kind of way or he may be just chilling lying flat on the sofa in his cozy flat underground beneath the Treble Staff.

🎨 Personalise Your Sharps and Flats

The best mnemonics are the ones that come from *your* imagination. Ask yourself:

- What would this character look like one step higher or lower?
- How would their energy or attitude change?
- What tiny detail can I exaggerate to make my mnemonic unforgettable?

You can sketch them, describe them, or simply imagine them vividly in your mind. This turns every note variation into a memory anchor that sticks for good.

🧭 Why It Matters

Thinking of sharps and flats as unique images — not as "C4 plus something" — trains your brain to recognise every scientific note name instantly. It's a powerful shortcut for:

- Faster mental mapping of your instrument
- Clearer understanding of where each note lives
- Quicker recall when reading or writing notation

And of course, once you've made those images second nature, they'll support your sight-reading, fingering, and ear training mnemonics automatically — part of the same system, just different layers of the map.

Quick Recap

This book helps you:

✅ Remember the scientific note names (C4, D5, etc.) easily.
✅ Anchor each one with vivid, playful imagery.
✅ Build a clear, colourful map of the musical landscape.
✅ Bonus: naturally improve pitch awareness along the way.

That's it — simple, creative, and designed for how memory really works. Now, let's meet your first scientific notes.

Colour Mnemonics - Key

amber for **A**

blue for **B**

crimson for **C**

damson for **D**

emerald for **E**

fawn for **F**

gold for **G**

E4 - the Elf note

Scientific Elves watch E4 every fortnight!

F4 - the Forest note

Scientific *fawns* frolic
with *formula* through the *Forest*

G4 - the Guitar note

Scientific Guitarists glitch
and *for*get the notes

A4 - the Apricot note

Scientists *inform* us Apricots are awesome *for* all

B4 - the Boxer note

Scientific Boxers tank up from water bottles *before* a battle

D5: the Donkey note

Scientific Donkeys work 9 to 5
(what a way to make a living)

E5: the Everest note

5 scientists eagerly explore Everest

F5: the Fudge note

Scientists *thrive* on Fudge at 5!

Scientific **Fudge** has **5** nuts per piece

Ledger Line Notes BELOW

D4 - the Digger note

Scientific Diggers *forge* ahead,
doing work on 4 wheels

C4 - the Castle note

Middle C

Scientific Castles are explosive - scientists inside them should not cook-up *formulas* with C4

B3 - the Bones note

*Free*zing scientists bring up buried **B**ones - wishing they hadn't volunteered at the burial site for *free*

A3 - the Ace note

The scientist's Ace appears on 3;
A flick of the wrist — pure mastery.

G3 - the Gold note

The scientific **Gold** owner has to run from *free*loading golddiggers

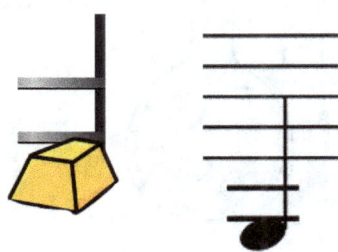

F3 - the Fish note

Scientific Fish swim on the
3rd ledger line below

E3 - the Equestrian note

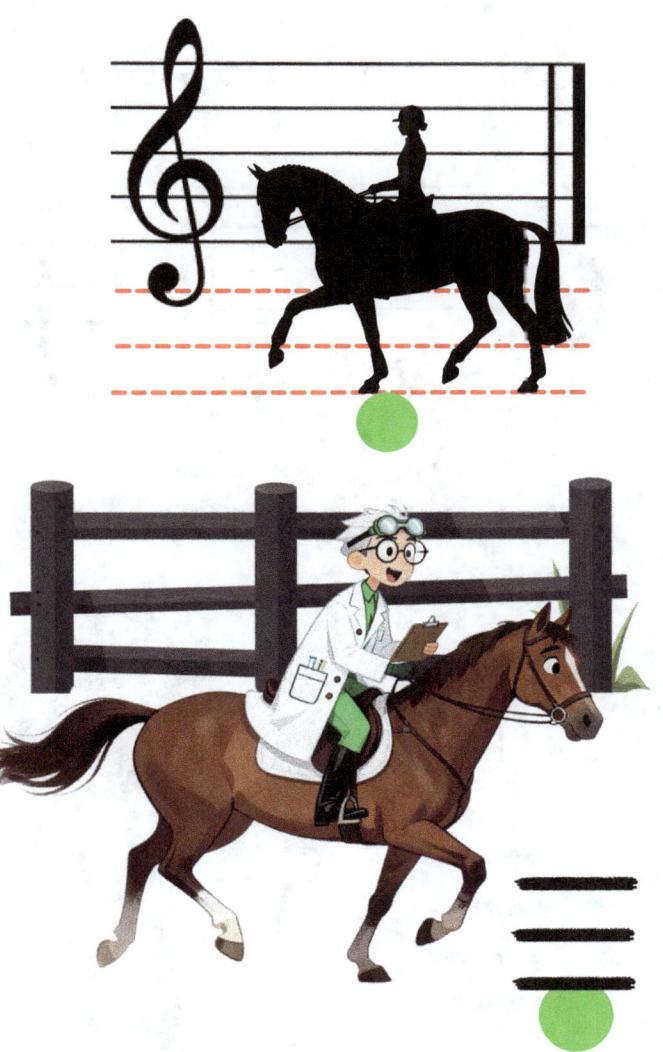

Scientific Equestrians ride *freestyle*

C3 - the Cart note

Scientific Carts career down aisles crammed full of *freaky* items

B2 - the Boat note

Scientists row Boats with 2 oars

A2 - the Armadillo note

2 Scientific Armadillos
have *to* argue analysing atoms

G2 - The Glue Note

Scientific Glue
is 2 fix things

F2 - the Farmer note

Scientific Farmers find they have 2 toil hard

E2 - the Emerald note

The scientific Emerald thief has **2** use a bunsen burner torch **2** see his way

Ledger Line Notes ABOVE

G5 - the Ghost note

Scientific Ghosts jive in Lab No 5

A5 - the Airplane note

The scientific Airplane flying to the conference has **5** scientists aboard

It's a 5-hour flight

C6 - the Comet note
the Scientific Comet looks like a 6

D6 - the Dog note

The scientific Dog has fetched 6 sticks for tricks

E6 - the Electricity note

The scientist's Electric device sparks at 6 v

F6 - the Falcon note

The scientific Falcon flies at **6** knots per hour

G6 - the Great note

Scientific Greats grapple with 6 theories!

A6 - the Alien note

Scientific Aliens activate 6 arms

B6 - the Band note

The scientific Band has roadies six;
Beavering hard setting up the mix
While each of them spins tunes 'n tricks.,

C7 - the Cannonball note

Scientific Cannonballs fire
ia 7-gun salute 7 days a week at 7 am

D7 - the Daughter note

The scientific Daughters of Professor Bevon;
Were 7 in number, and none named Evan.

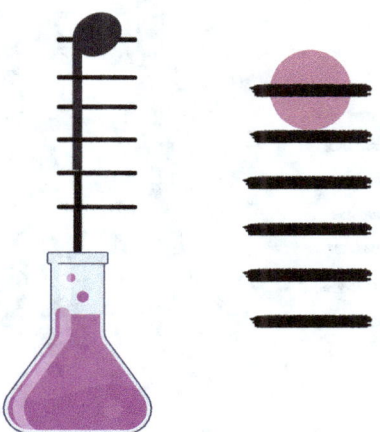

E7 - the Elevator note

Scientific Elevators go up to the 7th heaven

F7 - the Funfair note

Scientific Funfairs are open
7 days a week (also on 7th ledger line)

G7 - the Giant note

The scientific Giant danced on cloud 7,
Wearing socks that smelled like heaven!

A7 - the Ape note

The scientific Ape knows the secret chord to please the Lord!

"This monkey's gone to heaven!"

B7 - the Baby note

The high-pitched scientific Baby needs bottles & diapers 7 days a week!

C8 - the Crocodile note

The Scientific Crocodile *'ate'* in style

The highest pitch note on the piano as his dinner screamed very high pitched!

Treble Clef Notes

E2 - the Emerald note
F2 - the Farmer note
G2 - the Glue note
A2 - the Armadillo note
B2 - the Boat note
C3 - the Cart note
D3 - the Data note
E3 - the Equestrian note
F3 the Fish note
G3 - the Gold note
A3 - the Ace note
B3 - the Bones note
C4 - the Castle note
D4 - the Digger note
E4 - the Elf note
F4 - the Forest note
G4 - the Guitar note
A4 - the Apricot note
B4 - the Boxer note
C5 - the Car note
D5 - the Donkey note
E5 - the Everest note
F5 - the Fudge note
G5 - the Ghost note
A5 - the Airplane note
B5 - the Bee note
C6 - the Comet note
D6 - the Dog note
E6 - the Electricity note
F6 - the Falcon note
G6 - the Great note
A6 - the Alien note
B6 - the Band note
C7 - the Cannonball note
D7 - the Daughter note
E7 - the Elevator note
F7 - the Funfair note
G7 - the Giant note
A7 - the Ape note
B7 - the Baby note
C8 - the Crocodile note

The Bass Staff

G2 - the Goose note

The scientific Goose lays 2 glittering eggs

A2 - the Army note

The Army scientist had **2** amazingly ample burgers for lunch

B2 - the Bat note

Scientific Bats live on the 2nd line
and talk 2 much

C3 - the Cow note

Scientific Cows cowculate how much milk fills 3 churns

D3 - the Donut note

Scientist's Donuts are 3 lines up,
and eaten daily at 3

E3 - the Egg note

Scientific Eggs sit in the 3rd space up

The scientists analyse 3 main parts of the egg: the shell, the white & the yolk

F3 - the Fairy note

Scientific Fairies use the latest tech to grant wishes *free*ly

G3 - the Glasses note

Scientist's Glasses have lenses 3 times as strong

A3 - the Angel note

Scientific Angels hang up
A3-size posters on their walls

Ledger Line Notes BELOW

F2 - the Frog note

Scientific Frogs do tea for 2

E2 - the Earthworm note

Scientific Earthworms have erupting stomachs so have **2** dash to the loo

D2 - the Diver note

Scientific Divers have 2 document depth gauges

C2 - the Coal note

Scientific Coal miners cheerfully say "*toodaloo*"

B1 - the Badger note

Scientific Badgers ride bikes with only 1 wheel

A1 - the Ant note

Scientific Ants roll 1 ant ball

G1 - the Gas note

Scientific Gas flows through
1 pipeline to the lab

F1 - the Factory note

Scientific Factory workers drive to work in F1 cars!

E1 - the Easter Bunny note

Scientific Easter Bunnies only come out 1 time a year

D1 - the Disco note

Scientist's Discos have 1 dazzling disco ball

C1 - the Casket note

Scientist's Caskets are made for 1

BO - the Boombox note

The scientist with the Boombox has BO (Body Odour)

AO - the Aussie note

has no 'O' worries, mate!

**the lowest note on the piano...
way down under**

Ledger Line Notes ABOVE

B3 - the Butler note

Scientist's Butlers bring tea at 3

C4 - the Castle note

D4 - the Dragon note

Scientific Dragons take forty winks

E4 - the Ear note

Scientific Ears have 2 elegant earrings

F4 - the Fan note

Scientific Fans are *for* keeping labs cool

G4 - the God Note

Scientist God designed all 4 corners of the world

A4 - the Aster note

*Scientific Asters
grow 4-leaf
so are quite a relief*

B4 - the Brainy note

Brainy scientists are *fortunate*

It is also on the 4th ledger line up

C5 - the Climber note

Scientist Climbers use all **5** digits of their hands to grip the rock

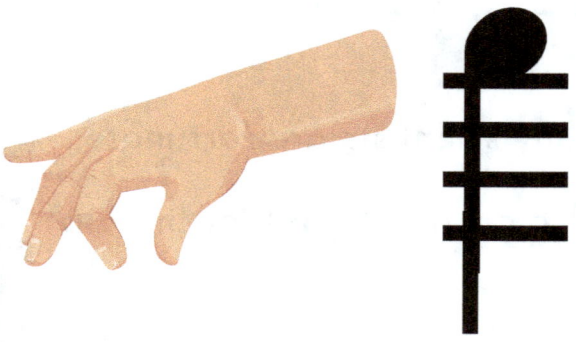

D5 - the Doodles note

Scientists Doodle 5 stars

E5 - the Emu note

F5 - the Football note

Scientists play 5-a-side football

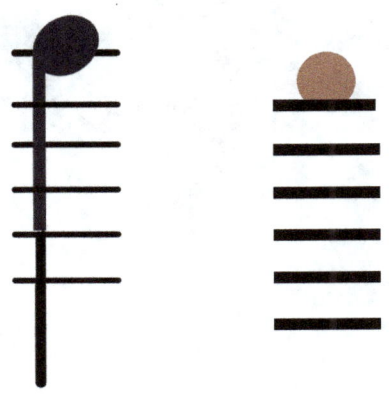

G5 - the Giraffe note

Scientific Giraffes gyrate 5 times

A5 - the Attic note

Scientists archive **5** antiques in their Attics

A0 - the Aussie note
B0 - the boombox note
C1 - the casket note
D1 - the disco note
E1 - the Easter Bunny note
F1 - the factory note
G1 - the gas note
A1 - the ant note
B1 - the badger note
C2 - the coal note
D2 - the diver note
E2 - the earthworm note
F2 - the frog note
G2 - the goose note
A2 - the army note
B2 - the bat note
C3 - the cow note
D3 - the donut note
E3 - the egg note
F3 - the fairy note
G3 - the glasses note
A3 - the angel note
B3 - the butler note
C4 - the castle note
D4 - the dragon note
E4 - the ear note
F4 - the fan note
G4 - the God note
A4 - the aster note
B4 - the brainy note
C5 - the climber note
D5 - the doodles note
E5 - the emu note
F5 - the football note
G5 - the giraffe note
A5 - the attic note

♠ About This Series: The Music Mnemonics System

Music is easier to remember when your brain actually enjoys learning it. That's the idea behind *Music Mnemonics* — a creative, story-driven approach to mastering every side of musicianship.

Each book uses consistent characters, colours, and memory hooks so your skills build naturally layer by layer:

🎵 Treble & Bass Clef Notes for Sight-Reading
Focus: Sight-reading
What you'll learn: Instantly recognise notes on the staff through story and image.

🧠 Scientific Note Names: SPN Hacks (this book)
Focus: Pitch naming
What you'll learn: Learn the scientific note names (C4, A5, etc.) through vivid mnemonics and colour cues.

🎹 Instrument Mnemonics Guides
Focus: Fingering & instrument mapping
What you'll learn: Connect your visual mnemonics to physical note positions on your instrument.

🎧 Ear Training Mnemonics
Focus: Aural skills
What you'll learn: Train your ear through the same characters and imagery you already know.

Each title works beautifully on its own — or as part of a complete memory-based learning system that transforms how you read, play, and hear music.

It's fun. It's fast. And it's designed the way your brain actually likes to learn — through imagination, pattern, and play.

www.ingramcontent.com/pod-product-compliance
Lightning Source LLC
Chambersburg PA
CBHW052107070526
44584CB00017B/2368